Charles of the Desert

A LIFE IN VERSE

Charles of the Desert

A LIFE IN VERSE

William Woolfitt

PARACLETE PRESS
BREWSTER, MASSACHUSETTS

2016 First printing

Charles of the Desert: A Life in Verse

Copyright © 2016 by William Kelley Woolfitt

ISBN 978-1-61261-764-0

The Paraclete Press name and logo (dove on cross) are trademarks of
Paraclete Press, Inc.

Other versions of "Sparrow Lament" and "Meditation on the Hands of an Ex-
Slave" appear in *Beauty Strip* (Huntsville, TX: Texas Review Press, 2014).

Library of Congress Cataloging-in-Publication Data
Names: Woolfitt, William Kelley, 1974– author.
Title: Charles of the desert : a life in verse / William Woolfitt.
Description: Brewster, Massachusetts : Paraclete Press, 2016. | Series:
    Paraclete poetry
Identifiers: LCCN 2015038774 | ISBN 9781612617640 (paperback)
Subjects: LCSH: Foucauld, Charles de, 1858–1916—Poetry. | Spiritual
    life—Poetry. | Christian poetry, American. | BISAC: RELIGION / Christian
    Church / History. | POETRY / Inspirational & Religious. | RELIGION /
    Christian Life / Prayer.
Classification: LCC PS3623.O723 C47 2016 | DDC 811/.6—dc23
LC record available at http://lccn.loc.gov/2015038774

10 9 8 7 6 5 4 3 2 1

Published by Paraclete Press

Brewster, Massachusetts

www.paracletepress.com

Printed in the United States of America

FOR MY PARENTS
Jim and Janie Woolfitt

Contents

Preface

I was on a Greyhound bus somewhere between Fairmont, West Virginia, and Bandera, Texas, when I first learned about Charles de Foucauld. It was the summer of 1997, I had just taken a job as a camp counselor, and I had borrowed a book at random from my church library—something to read during the two-day bus ride. The book was *The Signature of Jesus: The Call to a Life Marked by Holy Passion and Relentless Faith*, by Brennan Manning; I think that as I read it, I must have heard a still small voice, a gust of wind, a rusty gate creaking open. There was much about my new job that normally would have caused fear and worry and dread to well up in me; the camp director had told me little that would prepare me, other than that I would live in a canvas teepee without electricity, and that I needed old sneakers to wear in the Medina River. But Manning's book powerfully reassured me. I read about Abraham's journey by faith from Haran to Canaan, and Dietrich Bonhoeffer's embrace of the cross and martyrdom, and Charles de Foucauld's prayer of abandonment, and I forgot to be afraid. If my life had been a barred door, a nailed crate, a bricked-over cave, then that was the summer I began to wish I could be trusting and compassionate and servant-hearted. That was the summer the light started to get in.

I also started writing poems in 1997; my first poems tended to be autobiographical, sometimes angst-ridden and confessional, possibly navel-gazing and self-indulgent. Nine years later, I started to work on the project that would become *Charles of the Desert*. I was inspired by other poets who had taken biographical turns; I was reading Madeline DeFrees's *Imaginary Ancestors*, Andrew Hudgins's *After the Lost War*, Denise Levertov's poems about Julian of Norwich and Brother Lawrence and other historical figures, and Marilyn Nelson's *Carver: a Life*. I also chose poetry because it seemed the best vehicle to convey the expressions of prayer and penance and praise that characterize Charles de Foucauld's letters and journal entries, and because Charles collected and translated many Tuareg poems.

Once, I would have said that I was stepping away from the personal-autobiographical mode when my poems turned to the life of Charles de Foucauld; today, I am not so certain. I know that *Charles of the Desert* is a creative work that fictionalizes some details from the life of Charles de Foucauld; I also know that I may have made a version of Charles in my own image, so much so that I have tipped the scales toward autobiography all over again. Nevertheless, I hope that in some small way *Charles of the Desert* can carry on the work of Manning's *The Signature of Jesus* and de Foucauld's writings—the work of stirring the reader, calling to the heart, shaking loose and prying open, letting in the wind and the light.

~

In writing *Charles of the Desert*, I have relied on a number of books for facts, insights, and the occasional phrases I have borrowed or adapted. These include *Charles de Foucauld* by Jean-Jacques Antier; *Charles de Foucauld: Hermit and Explorer* by René Bazin; *Soldier of the Spirit: the Life of Charles de Foucauld* by Michel Carrouges; *Pilgrims of Christ on the Muslim Road: Exploring a New Path Between Two Faiths* by Paul-Gordon Chandler; *Charles de Foucauld: Writings*, edited by Robert Ellsberg; *Desert Calling: The Story of Charles de Foucauld* by Anne Fremantle; *Charles de Foucauld* by Pierre Lyautey; and *Witness in the Desert: The Life of Charles de Foucauld* by Jean-François Six.

My thanks to Mark S. Burrows, Jon M. Sweeney, and the staff of Paraclete Press for their belief in this work. Thanks, too, to Robin Becker and Charlotte Holmes, the best of first readers, and to Lisa Ampleman,

Sarah Blake, Kevin Brown, Katie Carlson, Lisa Coffman, Todd Davis, Brent House, Julia Spicher Kasdorf, Rachel Marie Patterson, Joshua Robbins, Chad Schrock, and Anya Silver. Thanks to Doris Kelley, Emmylou McDaniel, and Ethan Woolfitt. And my thanks to Sara for sharing with me life and "the dizzying multiplication of all language can name or fail to name."

I abandon myself into your hands;
do with me what you will.
Whatever you may do, I thank you:
I am ready for all, I accept all.

—*Charles de Foucauld*
1 8 5 8 – 1 9 1 6

Charles of the Desert
A LIFE IN VERSE

My Father as Weather Formation
∘ 1863 ∘
Wissembourg, France

Sometimes when a man moves his mouth, breath
comes out, breath that freezes in the prickly air,
only breath, no sounds. Like my father driving us
to the woods: me, baby sister, and mother, squeezed
beside him, shivering on the seat. Sometimes I look

and look at his whip-like body, his bulging eyes
that say to me he's half-lizard, his transformation
incomplete. I tell my sister, *his mouth makes no words,
only smoke.* My mother whispers, *chestnut, fir,
mirabelle* while my father veers from tree to tree.

He presses his hand to the bark, rips a leaf, scribbles,
picks a thread from his tweed coat (its sleeve
scours my cheek, becomes burlap in memory),
bites into a spotted plum, exposing the stone that glistens
like the pig hearts I saw, on tiptoe, at the butchery.

Then his whims enslave him. He stuffs his valise
with jars and papers, flees to the city. Mother blames
his fever, says he'll die. I dream he eats the char-
woman's lye to poison himself clean, soft
jellyfish man answering his gloom. Man of fidgets

and glances, soon to appear in the clouds as beasts
for me to name, and fall on his woods like snow.

My Mother as Harp Seal, as Sacristan

Wissembourg, France

In memory, she's still floating in the salted
bath, warmth gone from the gritty water
I ripple with my hand, her hair loose, adrift
over her body. White and quivering. Ask her
why she's sad again, she slides, goes under,
blows bubbles. With only her mouth and nose
out of the water, she says, *your brother,*
dead baby, you remind me, you have
his name. This I know for true: like a clump
of snow from a shaken branch, he fell
from her belly. In memory, spots of wet

on the floor. We had knelt that morning
to give daisies and asters, to kiss the feet
of the pale, poor eggshell man who hung
on the church wall, his weight webbing
cracks through the plaster. Ask her, *may we*
bring a blanket for him? On my bureau,
I still have a thumb of blistered wax, a string
of dead beetles. On my bureau, she's arranging
the candle and rosary. One hundred times I will
myself to remember the blanket I promised;
one hundred times, I forget.

The Children's Book of the Nativity

Father coughs into his sleeve, lives on pastries
and rain. Mother prays to the brass-eared saint,

miscarries, loses her joy, and then her life.
We are not safe, sister. We freeze while grandfather

inspects us, are there crumbs on our mouths,
jam on my trousers, dog hairs on your gown.

Steal for me, sister. He won't see. Not the cardboard
magi or ass, not the chestnut seller or fishwife.

You snatch the gilded china baby, then trip
over grandfather's cane. The babe shatters;

grandfather sends me to the yard. I shiver,
wait for his lashes to mark me, while he quakes

like a man waiting for grief to pass.

The House of Bones
○ 1873 ○
Nancy, France

Grandfather filled in as my father.
We lived in a repository of Roman coins,
pinned beetles, leather-bound books
that crumbled if touched. His brood
of friends—officers, scholars, priests—
clomped from room to room, applauded

his cases of animal skulls. Under a festoon
of cobwebs, I flaunted for them my Latin.
Carp-eyes ogled. Yellow teeth flashed.
I also despised the riverbed, the shale bluffs
he loved, where he took me to dig
fossils from a moraine. Home again,

cleaning up, the spade's handle
slivered into my hand. I squealed and thrashed;
he begged me to hold still, joined needle
to lit match, eased the splinter
from my smarting flesh.
His face paled, as it did the rare times

he spoke of mother. I tried a little test:
sob, sniffle, embellish. He gave me
bed rest, mulled wine, supper on a tray.
For years after that, I could get crayons,
good meat, candy, anything I wished.
Then grandfather turned on me, decided

I must attend the Polytechnic School
and join the army, so that I could kill
the Prussians who drove us from Strasbourg.
He said that I had mother's face,
that I should grow a moustache
to disguise my womanly mouth.

Red Coals

Grandfather hands me over to Saint Geneviève School,
the Jesuits. I fail my classes, write letters begging him
to let me come home, thirty pages or more.
The fathers freeze us all day, then gorge the stoves
with coal at bedtime, to stew us while we dream.

All the boys sweat beneath scratchy coverlets,
snug as dough in loaf pans, coverlets piled
like stones on the chest of Saint Victor.
Red-faced, I toss while I sleep, taste salt
when I lick the back of my hand.

We may not open windows, all the better to burn
the sin-inventing devils out of us. The fathers insist
they will straighten me. They apply fire, hammer,
and tongs until I take a new shape,
until I am molten, malleable, aglow.

Summer in Giverny

In my idle hands, I tossed the brigantine my cousin had folded in her exact way. I was staying at my uncle's chateau that sticky summer. I was sixteen; she was almost twenty. I had watched her slender fingers as she marked, creased, and flattened the boat she'd promised to shape, and as she perfumed her ears, wrists, and neck. When I asked her to resume the Italian lessons she'd taught me the summer before, she gave me a small painting: the Sacred Heart encircled with thorns.

⌒

For my confirmation, she had given me Bossuet's *Elevation of the Soul*. Flint struck steel. My faith rose like a tongue of flame, but I had nothing to feed it. My life was all green wood.

⌒

I stole Cousin Marthe's hair ribbons. I loaded her boat with ants, set it afloat on my uncle's pond, then angled a magnifying glass, filled the boat's paper folds with wisps of fire. Why did I feel the heat, as if I was catching the sun, weak as paper when it burns? After the boat sank, I shucked off my clothes, and dove into the pond. I stayed under. I watched the alchemy of displaced water—water that clouded as my toes wiggled, sunk into the ooze, and then stirred, and stirred.

Gold Eater

Give me fruits, spoils, fats, touches, tastes.
The buds of my tongue cry for mushrooms, pungent cheese,
magic foods charmed from the dark, delights slurped
or torn with teeth. I take, and take, and take.
I take from the bent man who crept the cellar stairs
each day to riddle the champagne bottle an eighth of a turn,
nudging it upside down to settle the cloud of dead

yeast cells in its wired neck. And from a goose
in a wooden crate (so small, she could not move);
she ate forced portions, never saw the sun.
Augers slid into an airhole (drilled in the crate's lid),
slid into her beak and craw; then kernels slid down
the auger's grooves, to stuff her gut, and pillow
her liver in golden fat. And hats, brooches, furs,

these I strip from the merchant's rack for Violette,
who ripped her hem the first June night she flitted
over my sill, laughing and moon-gilt. Violette poses
while I sketch her. I like her soft and naked as a bud.
I thumb the fat of her arm, count the time
before my mark fades. When she bores me, I try
horse races, quail, grouse, and buntings by the brace,

card games, and imported cigars. Violette rigs a beggar
costume that I will don to sneak away from officer duties.
We shutter the windows, stuff scarves under the door-crack
to banish the coming day. We stagger, topple two chairs,
our bodies prodigal and blind, my hand reading her face.

Cavalry Scene

∘ 1 8 8 1 ∘

Oran Province, Algeria

Enemies fire at us from the gullies of a nearby hill.
Black as a smashed toe when the tissue dies, smoke rises
in little funnels and swirls. I call on my Arabs to refresh

our bullets. No reply. I find them stretched face down
on the ground, body after body true as compass needles,
pointing to Mecca as they intone their prayers.

I scan the hill, its clumped weeds. The smoke fades;
our enemies also set aside their guns while they pray.
The sun spills liquid gold, and dips, and sways.

Quiet as a spider when it births silk,
I wish that I, too, could rest on the earth.

To Map the Land of God

Morocco

I grow sideburns. I buy robes, gowns, a yarmulke.
In the name of the Beneficent, the Merciful,
I rehearse the faltering Arabic of my alibi:
I am Youssef Aleman, a rabbi born in Russia,
fleeing from persecutions there.

Mardochée tugs my elbow, implores me
to let him speak. He's a genuine rabbi, bedraggled
and snuff-stained, the only guide I can afford.
He says, *forget your mapmaking dreams,*
or we'll both die.

The Koran and the Torah fill my mouth;
my teeth trip over new verbs.

Mardochée says to me, *why chance my life*
for your rude wage? He says, *snakes, fleas.*

I read: all good deeds
and acts of worship are for God.

Mardochée says, *it's not too late to change our plans*
and flee the caravan, or else, like fools, let us ride
south from Tangiers on these sickly mules. He says,
scorching days ahead; we may die a thousand ways,
following your map of wild guesses and blanks.

I cannot resist a land forbidden, unknown,
where Frenchmen are considered spies
and put to death, where faith is proclaimed
by the virile devotion of the Muslim man.
Rug weaver, silversmith, grower of figs, olives,
or cork; servant or slave—no matter his rank,
he ceases all motion, bows to the east
when the muezzin calls.

Mardochée says, *bandits, maggoty food,*
but like a Muslim I beseech, *peace be upon us,*
bestow favor, show the straight path.
The Rif Mountains crowd my dreams;
their jagged teeth rake the sky. I must juggle
two fruits, never drop or bruise them:
Arabic my muskmelon, Berber my pomegranate.

Villagers call us monkeys, spit at us,
hurl sharp stones and curses. I hide my notes
in my sleeves.

Mardochée says, *reconsider; we must turn back.*
I say, *not without finishing the map.*

Gourd Seeds

○ 1 8 8 6 ○
Paris, France

The travelogue I publish, ample material
for the nests of silverfish that nibble and corrupt.
The gold medallion I win,

would trade to know that God exists.
I grin at the rabble of acclaim, pile the showy
words, then gnaw them, suck down the marrow.

I take Marthe's little sons to a mound of pebbles,
teach them to dig shards of pottery and bone,
and steal them from her in my dreams.

I woo the topographer's daughter,
give her a small cautious kiss.
With all these nothings to adorn me,

I rooster-strut the streets of Paris,
my chest medaled, my feathers ruffed
because I possess the skill of transporting

mountains from eye to map.
Self-appeasements pour from my lips.
I clamor with the rubbish wagon

as it passes by, and resound with the carillon
of the liturgy, and chew the quick
when friends turn my doorknob again

and again; I rattle with the seeds
trapped in gourds, begging for liberty,
for soil and sun.

The Pangs of Wanting

Paris, France

I want to explore unmapped lands; meditate on deep truths;
argue with shrewd, brilliant men; make love to a woman

versed in the pieties of faith and the pleasures of the earth;
try celibacy; father able sons. To my nephews, Pierre

and Andre, I distribute my soldier and rabbi costumes:
waistcoat, plumed hat, boots, scimitar, turban, burnoose,

scabbard, blue slippers. May all the trappings of those lives
serve as their playthings. I deliver my body to the church,

though I cannot imagine what penance might relieve
these pangs of wanting. I beg Father Huvelin to direct me.

I say, *I long to have faith.* I take first communion
for the second time in my life, husk who lived as a swine.

I lift my chin. My tongue licks up the bread: a whisper
of paper on my teeth, a morsel of dust, molecule-thin.

I gulp vinegar, dark, smoky, acidic, then sweet, garnet
and carnelian, the cup reflecting the candle flame,

pelting me with stars. His torn body in my stomach,
his blood in my spit, I almost vomit; I almost sing.

At the Ruins of Pilate's Palace

∘ 1 8 8 8 ∘
Jerusalem

Seeking relics, old tombs, rumors of bone,
I come to the pretorium's ruins, rubble
choked with clock-flower vines. I blow grit

from the mosaic stones where the prefect stood
the day he proclaimed that he found in Christ
no wrong, then dipped his fingers into the dish,

flung drops of water far from his spidery hands,
gave Christ to the throngs. I press my hand, groove
my skin with the grains of the paving stones.

Tether

Ardèche, France

Then I practice frozen lips,
tongue of lead. I shed cravings,
peel away the encumbrances

of the body. The older monks eat
without sound; soften the swish
of robes; step with feet that feather

the earth. My spoon clatters. Phlegm
rattles my lungs. I pray that prayer
can tether me, be the cool

gray stone that dulls my rough edges
and burrs. After High Mass, I turn
to chores: I pull thistles, rub the brass,

gather kindling, twine wreaths,
thresh and bundle the hay.
Small interruptions are savored.

The yipping fox. The blue rock-thrush
who pipes the same six notes.
In my free hour, I read the breviary,

nurse my sore feet, dig my thumb
between the long bones and tendons,
and remember that I am foul matter.

Automaton with Flute

Akbès, Syria

I am still a man of parts, fractions, halves,
a copper weathercock that wavers, dips
in the smallest wind. I am still Vaucanson's

fluteur automate, imitation of a living man,
cannot compress my lungs, open my lips
or sound a note, unless other hands work my bars,

levers, and bellows. My soul stays timorous,
cold, a flint that gives no sparks; my prayers
spill like gears from my unfastened mouth.

Obedientiary

We fan out, we fall into line. Alongside the next rock that juts from the earth, we squat, we thrust fingers into the dirt-seam. Alongside the irregular and craterous, the quartz-flecked, we grasp, we pry and tug.

Brother Raoul, thin as a filament, struggles with a rudder-shaped stone, and falls hard, scrapes open his knee. Bearing the stone once more, he marches, his head veiny, blue-webbed; his eyes joyed, fever-bright.

In silence, he reminds us to give thanks for all our gifts: perseverance that combs our snarls and loose threads, that we might be spun, shuttled, woven into lasting cloth. Patience that sinks me deeper here, entombing me, true as a tap-root, in the last place I long for.

I free the next stone, and strain, lift it to my chest. Across the field, dodging the uneven sockets that held stones we plucked out, to our wall that rises each day. Incremental. Steadfast. We stand in line, we scatter.

We pass our stones to the abbot. He sizes each stone, seeks a good fit.

Hornet Swarm as the Sins of Mankind

○ 1 8 9 5 ○

Akbès, Syria

This is the dream:
people surround me, taunt and sneer,
buzz like horseflies, throw elbows, shove against,
straining to glimpse the convicts, the soldiers
prodding them down the street. I see two thieves
limp and plod, then comes blasphemy-made-flesh—
all three scourged, bloody and staggering as they drag
the posts they will writhe upon. I see Simon of Cyrene
swept along like seaweed in an ebb-tide, then I am Simon,
stepping toward the street, I take another step,
forget that I know what happens next.

This is still the dream:
the jeerers freeze, their hiss and yammer dies out,
silenced by a droning keen, a cloud of specks that darkens
half the sky, then veers, comes closer, lands on him
who calls himself temple raiser, true vine. Masses of hornets
slip into his skin, plug his wounds, and stanch the bleeding
for an instant, then sink into him, like cloves
stuffing a rice pudding.

I think I'm starting to wake:
the sin-glutted man jerks like a marionette,
his body swells, and balloons, and shrinks back down.
Simon's hand buffets the air, my hand
bunches the sheet, Simon can't see
the cloud of hornet-specks,
but I feel the evil
in the gooseflesh on my arms,
the sparks in my hair.

The Hamidian Massacres

Up from Alexandretta and the sea, up in the Amanus Mountains, smoke gauzes the sky. Gunshots ring. We number our days. The lark weaves her twig-nest and warms her eggs, darts among the thorns of our bramble wall—the only defense we ever wanted for our monastery, a hedge against the bears. We tend the chalice and paten, the donkeys, milk-cows, and orphan children. Prayers billow from our cells in the hay-loft. Messages from our neighbors numb us more each day. Hamid the Butcher gives commands; the army loots and burns villages, severs hands and arms and lips, slaughters Armenians by the thousands, spills blood like mop water, stacks bodies like firewood. Refugees cram the cities, boil grass and bark for soup. I go to the fence to pray. The thorns splay like the fingers of a thousand desperate men; pierce the waxy, green-gray leaves; punish my curious hand like the teeth of a carnivorous fish.

Turkish guards keep us safe, coddled like glass princes in a velvet case. They hem us in, insisting that European monks be spared, death stays out, our mercy stays in. I patch the orphans' clothes, teach them a cherished verse: *we give our spirits into Your hands.* The sun slumps behind a dry, hot haze. I write letters to Marthe, my sister, our family lawyer, and Father Huvelin. I tell them the rumored numbers of the starving, the poxed, the dead. Send money, I say. Tell your newspapers, make any noise you can, write letters, bang a spoon against a pan.

Village Martyr

Akbès, Syria

In a smoky room with boarded windows,
the postmaster's son trembles, his leg-stumps
turning to ooze. His teeth clack like spoons

as his mother and I pray a few simple words.
I could give him the sacraments,
if I were a priest. His sister plucks

a bony stork for the stewpot, chops three
thumb-sized parsnips. His mother wrings
a thin rag, moistens the tip of his tongue.

Blue Aster

Flee from the vows. Go among trumpet gentians
and fire lilies, take from the high hidden field one aster,
sleeping blue star. Become a hermit laborer, give away

Brother Alberic's tidy habit, put on the threadbare blouse
and trousers of Charles the peasant. Press the aster
in the tiny antique book, gospel of the beloved, pouched

and hanging against the chest. Sail to Jaffa,
coast of Palestine, for eight days walk the road-ruts,
blistered, crumb-fed, footsore. Flower that mothers call

little queen marguerites. Picture the Eternal walking here,
bearing the cross on His back like an ox loaded
with timbers. From a relic seller, buy a nub of the sponge

lifted to the Eternal's parched lips, keep it near the aster,
faded blue. On St. Colette's Feast, arrive in Nazareth,
come upon the Poor Clares' Convent, kneel with them

in their chapel for the Exposition of the Blessed Bread.
When the sisters leave for supper, offer to keep watch
for the one who stays back to linger with the sacred bread.

Put a brittle blue petal on the altar, adore the *corpus Christi*
while a sister cracks the door, thinking she will catch
a tramp who means to steal the silver vessels and tray.

Offer to work for the mother superior as a handyman.
When she pinches her nose, brings a pail of water
and soap that stings, give her the filthy clothes;

keep from her the dear book, the aster, snuffed blue dust;
let water move over skin, a lavish hand. For wages,
take the hovel behind the convent that sleeps one

with a pillow of stone, used papers for meditations
and letters, mustard greens and heels of bread.

Liturgy of the Hours (i)

○ 1 8 9 7 – 1 8 9 8 ○
Palestine

Remover of rough stones that rise
from her flowerbeds, herbalist who thins dill
and creeping thyme, Mother Mary of St. Michael
cares for whoever raps at her gate.
"Take some soup, not just the coarse bread,"
she whispers, hand over mouth, her voice
a puff of air. "Let us provide what you require."
I share her toolshed with the hoe and the rake,
sleep on my side, curled like a leaf. I need
no soup, no mother. At vigils, my dark prayers,
a vine sprouts from my mouth.

In the dark, a word comes to me, tiny sprout,
moss on a moon-washed stone. I kneel
in the sheepfold between my shed and the ravine.
When the bell rings for Lauds, I enter the chapel,
creep down to the cave that sheltered the Holy
Family when Jesus was a boy. I write meditations
all morning. I see him at five shaping clay into
animals, growing fast at fifteen, all gratitude,
no greed. I burn my hours, lay pride on the coals.

～

Full of greed, I hoard my hours, live as a hermit,
spurn my neighbors, refuse to help or be helped,
do not serve, hide behind prayer. When he visited
his parents in the cave, Jesus bent in the doorway
to not bruise his head. A solemn lesson: submit,
grow small. At Terce, I walk the road, give apricots
and nuts to the boys who taunt me; I pass my clothes
to the market beggars. I withdraw to the hills,
dig slips of lilies and loosestrife for the mothers'
flowerbeds, and bring pails of manure.

Although I weed, carry manure, the turnips wither.
My stone wall crumbles. I fail to shoot the jackal
that kills Mother Elisabeth's hens. Still, I try
to sow love in whomever I meet. Mother tells me,
of much use to God can be *a day, a grain of sand,*
a spider's web, a gardener whose cucumber blights
on the vine, an ex-monk too stubborn to become
a priest. All things add to the kingdom, she says—
even my melons, which are mealy, not sweet.

King of Hush

Nazareth

King of hush, king of hidden things,
of blood pulsing through veins and arteries,
king of fresh yeast, and salt, and sprouting seed,
the dog-woman's crumbs, the lost son's ring.

Slave of the stick's thud and the whip's sting,
slave of fall on your face and slump in the street,
of whimper and grunt, slave of creeping things,
of blood leaking and pebbles biting into knees.

Lover fallen like a star, trampled but lighting
the woman who poured her tears on your feet,
men who reek of sardines, boat-pitch, and the sea,
sandpiper eggs and the first frog in the spring,
small voices, foolish things.

Confessions of an Illuminator

○ 1 8 9 8 ○
Nazareth

Mother Elisabeth holds an envelope that I recognize.
She speaks to me through the varnished grill
that pours rhombuses of shadow and light
over her furrowed cheeks and tulip bulb nose.
I prepare to admit: thorns in my garden, the jackal
killed another hen, and I produce too much mail,

pounds a year; I squander ink, devour paper scraps,
 my stamps outnumber the grasshoppers in a plague.
Mother Elisabeth mentions not one of these charges.
She points to the iris I embellished on the flap, asks
if I will fill her chapel with scenes to inspire her nuns
when they pray: saints blooming from clematis vines,

the stations of the cross. The sister portress brings
boards, brushes, tubes of topaz-blue and cerulean,
Indian yellow, flame-red. I have not painted
for nine years. The first paint-drop I squeeze out
quivers and gleams like a tiny let-there-be.

Liturgy of the Hours (ii)

I try to live on God's words, pure and sweet—
but a new hunger howls in me, churns my guts:
the Mount of Beatitudes is for sale. I write my sister,
wanting my inheritance back. Like a snake
digesting a rat, I bloat with plans: *a tabernacle*
to build on that hill, then pilgrim crowds needing a priest
like me. I ask the mothers for counsel. They say,
ponder God's laws, God's ways. A dead tooth
falls from my gums; I can't chew bread.
My tongue sneaks back to check the empty spot.

～

The sisters will find an empty spot in the shed
where I slept. I must give up, flee, *throw myself
among the Beloved's friendless children.* As a priest,
I'll carry the spirit in my thoughts, my marrow,
my least cells. Let Mother Elisabeth remember me
as a thread of candle smoke. After the morning bell,
I will go forth. First, I must water the sisters' herbs,
paint ferns on their walls, sweep the chapel floor.

Ferns at the ravine's lip, a stream in its floor,
cool waters out of reach, the ravine-walls too steep,
wastrel moon lighting each sheep-chewed blade
and fern. *Shadow-wings, still night, perfect end,*
the rest of the compline that I cannot chant.
Each holy word a chestnut burr in my mouth.
Stream that fills the star-refracting pools.
God is not in my shed, the chapel, or the cave,
but near the good thief, the poor, the least ones,
the disowned I'll go to, the discarded stones.

Memento

Nazareth

Mopping the sisters' chapel
and parlor for the last time,
I decide I will take in secret
and keep for always, like a lock
of hair or a pressed anemone,
the voice of Mother Elisabeth,
as I remember it. Appraising,
cajoling, and knowing me,
she spoke through the black
curtain that hung between us.
In her grave laughter, I hear
a pail splash into a well,
a starling squabble when it finds
silver in a pile of stone.

Dust and Oil

° 1 9 0 1 °

Cathédrale Saint-Vincent, Viviers, France

Like a spruce hit by wind and lightning,
the bishop sways, crackles before me.
He charges me with the volts of his hands

clamped on my head, the singe of peace
he kisses to my brow. As the censer's flames
smoke and hiss, the floor tilts like the deck

of a ship. I sprawl at the bishop's feet,
hide my face, dizzied by the litany of saints.
May I discard the hermit's private joys:

living as dust that drifts into corners, cracks,
ditches, and ruts; hours lost in the delicious
adoration of God. I wear robes tailored

by Marthe, her gift of miniscule stitches
and linen like meringue, like folds of snow,
her embroidery, the cross, circlet of gold,

and crimson heart over my breast.
May I take the sacraments to the heart
of the Sahara, the unknown, the uttermost;

where there are no priests, may I offer
fraternal love to the soldiers of France,
may I prepare a feast for peasants,

nomads, and slaves. The bishop
consecrates my hands with chrism oil.
Which is the toucher, which the touched?

All mixed up, our four hands gleam,
drip, and ooze, like the boy's sardines
commandeered for the multitudes.

Changeling

I wish to accustom all the inhabitants, Christians, Muslims, and Jews, to look upon me as their brother, the universal brother. . . . They begin to call my house the fraternity (the zaouïa *in Arabic), and I am delighted.*

The rat snarls at me, skitters
through the rotten orange
flesh of the pumpkin that slid

from my hands, splatted
on the chapel floor. I wake
to the lowest place, the Cinderella life.

My visitors ask for barley, calico,
medicine, lodging, lost property.
As the door shudders, creaks,

swings open, I sweep out
the sand that gusts back in
all the broken day. My work

is to pray, serve, sweep, scurry
to the door, split and portion out
whatever is dear, breakable,

surplus—to soldiers, travelers,
beggars, slave hunters, runaways,
slave boys and girls, sons

and daughters kidnapped from Chad,
Tuat, Sahel. Each of us is a changeling,
certain to shrink and curl

like twists of burnt paper,
unless kindness bursts through
our lizard scales and mouse fur,

bidding each to grow, unfurl,
roam the earth as an enlarged
and marvelous creature.

For Three Hundred Francs

∘ 1 9 0 2 ∘
Béni Abbès, Algeria

I bought a slave boy this morning.
His old master untied his hands,
with monkey-fingers plucked, teased,
raveled the knots apart, saved the rope
for future use. Cord of all kinds is precious here;
we don't cut unless we must. The boy seized
my hand, clung to me like vines tangling a stake.
I called him Jean. I think he is about fifteen.
I know I must not overwhelm him with gifts.
Tunic, cloak, and slippers tomorrow;
for tonight, his own earthen cell
in the honeycomb of rooms
behind the palm chapel.

I bring Jean water and millet gruel.
He lets me watch him eat: slurp, gulp,
wheeze, shake, won't look up, brow pocked,
eyes lost. His master deemed him cheap,
and I cannot afford to free the able-bodied.
He winds the clock, lights the petroleum lamp,
folds tarps, carries a few stones to the low wall
that encloses the fraternity. Seizures tell
his biography: masters wrote lashes
over his back, blows upon his head.
His palsy will falter him to the grave;
for now, it curses him free.

We Hide Our Faces from the Wind

○ 1 9 0 3 ○
Béni Abbès, Algeria

If the Pères Blancs send money,
I will ransom more slaves. Jean, now free,
believes that the wind pursues him; he crouches
in burrows, old wells. We plug our ears

when the wind sputters and moans. I hear
the panting of boys with bands of scar
and bruise on their backs, two colors of tattoo.
Jean says the wind of harmattan burns

his ankles, his neck. The wind of simoom
flings sand at our hut, and scours the mothers
who lose their babies to thieves, and hardens
their tears to shards of salt, slivers of glass.

Meditation on the Hands of an Ex-Slave

o 1903 o
Béni Abbès, Algeria

Nails split, he cups
his hands to his chest,
hides the seams that cross

his palms, scar-lines
of labors for his master,
knives whetted, fires fed.

He clenches them
like tree buds—never open,
always spring.

The space inside them,
so near his heart,
must be holy—formless, empty,

dark as the face of the deep
waters, where the spirit hovers
before it calls out the light.

Oasis Prayers

Béni Abbès, Algeria

I assisted at Mass. His chapel, miserable corridor on columns, covered with rushes! A board for altar; for decoration a piece of calico with a picture of Christ; tin candlesticks; a flattened sardine tin with two bottles that once held mouthwash, for cruets and tray. —GENERAL HUBERT LYAUTEY

Young Joseph, strong as a palm beam, never completes
one chore; his hands evade. I remind him that he is free,
he may leave, but he sings hymns off-key, drowns me out.
He likes his life here, with Jean and Marie,

rooming in the fraternity. Marie, my only convert,
ancient and blind, kneels in the palm chapel all day.
Jean creeps behind me, stares as I serve bread and wine
to the sharpshooters, the commandant and his aide.

I tell these three that freeing them isn't enough.
We must pray for francs, for the thousands to be freed;
pray that fetters unfasten, that Europe intervenes,
that my purse fattens, that I might make more purchases;

pray that money comes from Marthe and my sister,
from the dole of the Pères Blancs, the Missionaries
of Our Lady of Africa, from the officers at the fort.
Marie, Joseph, and Jean nod at my babble,

perplexed by my speech. Language cloisters me.
I am a novice of desert tongues. We must draw
figures in the sand, or gesture. Our hands become
strange birds, pulling new shapes from the air.

Sparrow Lament

You fall, sparrow egg, God-eyed leaf,
black hair of ox, kernel of wheat,
gold blown from the stalk. You lift wood,
trudge, and lurch, your back pulped. You would
spit up the cup-dregs for relief—

but no, you want not; you believe
your master's dream. You toss your dreams
like chaff to the breeze. You lift wood.

You fall,

    thin coin,

        widow's all,

            copper seed

into the mouth of the box. She
brushed you a hundred times, so good
to hold, but better to drop. Wood
weights you, snapped bone, wind-flung leaf.

Flight Lines

○ 1 9 0 5 ○
Béni Abbès, Algeria

I must give up the palm grove and the bitter
coffee I grind from date-pits, my chapel
in the shadow of the fort, greenfinch
and bunting who crack seeds while I pray,

whatever I hold too long, want too much,
stones I pile to mark my hours as mine,
not my neighbors' to overrun. I will become the first
priest to live in Tamanrasset and study the Tuareg,

nomadic Muslims, men who carry amulets,
wear head-veils that stain their faces blue,
women who dance ecstatically, pound drums
made of antelope hide, go bare-faced. I hope

the good news flourishes like bunch-grass
spreading everywhere after rain. In that rocky land,
I'll eat the Eternal's food and live on air,
be freightless, open-handed, finch-boned.

Body as Pomegranate Tree
° 1905 °

To slay vanity, I test the hairshirt
of hunger, soothe with siftings of barley
three times a day; the sackcloth of desert

sun leathers my face and parches my eyes.
I meditate on the staggers and falls
of Jesus, mortified so that he might

embrace all men. The nettles of sleeping
unrobed in the black sand pock my skin
with pearls of grit. The flagellations

of the alarm clock's cry wrench me awake
to pray the divine offices in the deeps
of night with dull lips and a fogged brain.

I crucify the sinful flesh, as men drive
crows from the orchard with torches and stones.

The Rope Maker

Tamanrasset, Hoggar, Algeria

The dry bed of a wide river crosses the plateau of Tamanrasset. Charles built his oratory and hut near the left bank. All around was undulating stony ground, in which grew tufts of hard grass and guettaf, whitish salt-worts, a yard high; in a word, poor camel pasture. Within three miles, the solid mass of the Kudiat rises up dominated by the Ilaman peak, bare, heaped-up and rocky, colored by the sun toward evening with rose or fawn, with dark purple tints, undimmed by mist or dust. —RENÉ BAZIN

Dear Beatrix,

I think of our childhood together as I start afresh here in Tamanrasset. The Tuareg are nomadic, a people going or gone. In their eyes, I'm untrustworthy, friendly with French soldiers, I pray to a fickle god, I'm a colorless grub.

Do you remember when we first lived with Grandfather, how he seemed cold, and stiff, and severe? Then he sang off-key to amuse us, flapped his arms, won us over with silly opera arias, the song of Musette. I hope to coax the Tuareg bit-by-bit. I've visited their pastures and outlying camps, offered bread, played the buffoon for the children to laugh.

The man eager to give all—his crusts, his shoes, his pride—cannot be robbed.

Today, a woman motioned for me to squat beside her, the first Tuareg to chance that I am kind. She showed me how to soften date palm leaves and acacia bark in a basin of water. We ripped strands from the wet pulp, sat and extended our legs, flattened and pinched the strands.

Imagine my big toe sticking up like the stylus on a sundial; then my big toe becomes the spindle where Lalla stretches and loops the length of our rope as it plays out, strengthens, expands.

Christmas at the Frigate (i)

Tamanrasset, Hoggar, Algeria

Dear Beatrix,

A happy Christmas to you. Please don't send more baby dolls—your gifts of thread and soap better suit the clever Tuareg women. The old ladies seized the porcelain dolls, swatted the girls away. They lift cups of tea to the dolls' sealed mouths, dribble sticky liquid down rigid faces; they sew charms to frilly doll-dresses, mumble spells for fertility and rain.

I've received no other mail this month, few guests. Blame the cold weather. Rags on their backs, no fat on their bones, my neighbors huddle in their tents, use spears to dig up the sand, and burrow deep. I'm much too cozy here in the Frigate, walled by stone and red mud.

I trust you helped your children unpack the crib, fill it with straw, and tie stars of foil to the tree, as Grandfather once helped us, sowing us with his faith and discipline. He plucked out stones that bruise, weeds that choke. I still feel his shovel blows, how each strike tills and uproots, exposing me to the air and the light.

The Skin of a Viper's Jaw Transfigured

Tamanrasset, Hoggar, Algeria

Shaded by boulders, cooling my feet
in dark sand, I brush my arch against

a yellow rope that shudders, rises up
to strike. I see scales like jewels,

then light pouring through
the delicate skin of its hinged jaw

as it kisses my heel. Ragged heat
washes through me. I taste India rubber,

and petals of blood leak from my nose,
I fall, my bones melt, and I become

a sack of jelly. Then there is no viper.
I am alone. None to ease my thirst,

scratch my name in stone, lie near me
in my grave. Then the Tuareg shepherd

carries me to Dassine's tent, and anoints
my wound with red iron, lashes a strap

around my ankle, burns my foot again.
I smell my flesh cooking, I vomit,

drowse, and drink the potions
Dassine brings. I sleep, sail to France

and see my mother rip a lace shawl.
When I wake, I sit up, eat clots

of sour milk from Dassine's spoon.

Words for Flesh

Tamanrasset, Hoggar, Algeria

I cannot sketch the Tuareg, fail to catch
the departing backs of men on camels,
gone in a flash, racing for pasture and trade.
And if I studied the warbling women
who tend goats by day, who play

hide-drums and one-string violins,
dance slack-breasted when the sun bleeds
the black crags red, I would have to pluck
the lust from my eyes. When careless,
I find myself humming their tunes

instead of the psalms. I assemble a grammar,
a dictionary; I translate Tuareg poems,
the Gospels. My first words include *bowl,*
milk, and *moon, star, eye,* and *fire,* and *ash.*
Dassine, my tutor, governs the local Tuareg

when her uncle rides away. She passes
to the women my sewing notions, medicines,
and health advice. We trade words,
from her language to mine, and back again.
I mangle the Tifinagh script. Her warm hand

guides my hand. I try, try,
smudge the words I fail to shape.

Seed Speck, Tuber Eye

∘ 1 9 0 6 ∘

Tamanrasset, Hoggar, Algeria

My friends charm wells, gather dates,
store faith in tiny bulb, seed speck,
tuber eye. They farm the parched,
unarable. Scab-lipped, slur-bearers,
they keep secret, unpronounceable,
their true name, forcing me to say
"Haratin"—dark, dirty, foul,
if Dassine is right. They peddle
scrawny vegetables to Tuareg buyers
who point, back away, never touch.

Descended from slaves, they could go
anywhere, but stay—as do I. Nights here
spur me to praise the maker
of desert skies, starred with the blinking
eyes of my dead ones, sheltered by God's
sickle-shaped wings.

Christmas at the Frigate (ii)

Dear Beatrix,

I must thank you heartily for yesterday's package. I will divide its contents with the few families who are near. The Tuareg women may whistle for their goats, drive them to the scrub-grasses that thrive on rocky slopes; the Tuareg men may ride away on caravan; I always have the Haratin with me. The Haratin raise millet and sorghum, must know some secret art that coaxes crops to grow from slabs of stone.

I pray that the Haratin see me as brotherly and mild. I distribute to them carrot and turnip seeds; thank you for providing such a perfect gift. And thank you for the needles and manicure scissors, which have set the Haratin women all abuzz; their custom is to sew with a tool like a long curved thorn. The young men are knitting cardigans, and the grandmothers love you for sending black dye; they believe it returns beauty to their silvery nests of hair.

Brother Almost

At last, a fellow-monk says that he will
come to me: Raphael of the flaxen hair,
dainty lips and facial twitch, many sneezes
and groans, who gives me this pledge:
"I have no other course." We ride the train
to Colomb-Béchar, then walk south,
into the desert. Each day, he mumbles
and fades. He winces at the scalding light;
when I teach him to mix ink from charcoal
and camel piss, he clamps his nose.

∽

*I imagine Raphael embracing his vocation
and his life with me: he perks up when he joins
my work, lodges in my mud-house, becomes
with me a Targui, that we might gain the Tuareg.
He imitates me, becomes all things to all men,
words living in skin. The server's duties pink
his cheeks; for the good of me and all the Tuareg,
he arranges the water and the wine; at last,
I am permitted to say Mass again.*

Stomach cramps halt Raphael at In Salah.
He turns back. He never sees the dear
Hoggar tableland, the leather
tents of the Tuareg pitched among
scant grasses and sand pools,
the frozen lava fans, basalt turrets
and heaps of metamorphic rock,
proof that all things change.
To return home, I must cross
the Tanezrouft, the last and worst desert,
where nothing lives or grows.

Consider the Ant

○ 1 9 0 9 ○

Tamanrasset, Hoggar, Algeria

No rain, the *wadi* dry for months, its side channels
thin to veins of dust. Its bottom-stones crack like eggs.
The Tuareg pack their tents, drive their goats to graze
in far fields. On my walks, I sometimes find miracles

of food: acacia pods I can pound into edible meal;
once, a jerboa I stoned and dressed
for the roasting-spit; once, a snarl of bees
flitting from the mouth of a dead jackal,

and inside the carcass's dark cave, enough honey,
sweet and glistening, to fill the bowl of my hands.
This morning, I ask the Eternal to show me
an ant-hill rising from the stony ground,

rations to share with the Haratin. I am too sluggardly
to consider the ant and her wise ways, to take pains
to do good to the Haratin whenever I may.
The ant treasures the seeds of *tullult* grass,

hoards them in her tunnels. When I find an ant-hill,
I invite the Haratin children—a few, at least—
to dine on *tullult* seed porridge prepared by me,
pestle-lifter, earth eyer, bandit among the ants.

Skin Tent

In the tent of forty-two goat skins
cured with butter and red ochre,
the cheek-sucking grandmothers
hum and sway. Black teeth, rotten eyes,
hair falling out, last wisps of flesh

melting by the day, they lean forward,
hug the peaks of their knees with arms
like wreaths of bone. They rasp poems
about courtship parties, boys whipping
their camels across the plateau to woo

and caress moon-ripened girls. They laugh
as I scribble. *Why write? We remember.*
We always have. I give the grandmothers
safety pins, milk powder, the only food
I can provide. How will I tell them

Bread of Life, Pearl of Great Price?
Let my life be a poem, repeated
among them through space and time.

Desert Bath at Sunset

○ 1910 ○
Tamanrasset, Hoggar, Algeria

I wash my head with a splash
of water, scrub with sand
till the dead skin sloughs from my limbs.
I cup elbows, scratch belly,

scrub shoulder-blades with sand.
I squat down, cradle my toes.
I brush off elbows, belly,
remember the last bone

of soap that slivered between my toes,
and all else that I let go—
hearth embers, silver, beef bones.
Through the holes in my body

left by each letting go,
the red sun beams its light.
Giver of skin, hair, bodies,
whatever is good, I will not despise

what you give. Your bruise-red sun
embers the tamarind tree.
For your delight,
take my breath, fingers, bones, blood.

I lean on the lone tree.
Wind soughs through its crooked limbs,
promises me water and blood,
stinging rain, bread speckled with ash.

Teresa of Avila Compares the Soul to a Palm Cabbage

○ 1910 ○

Tamanrasset, Hoggar, Algeria

The soul is a conglomerate of crystals, Teresa wrote,
a castle of many rooms. My soul is not clear, or orderly,
or grand, but earth-enamored, cluttered, and black—
black as basalt, black as the whip-stitched threads

that bind and the stains that mar this notebook
I've sewn from old envelopes and paper scraps.
My sweat discolors its pages, as do the oils
of the many hands that deliver my mail.

Upon these uneven pages, I gather the notes
that I treasure: weather patterns, Tuareg proverbs,
well surveys, the uses of camel's milk, and hide,
and hair. And again, *the soul is a palm cabbage;*

she peels it, finds the kernel where God lives.
Here in Tamanrasset, the earth is a malicious father,
giving us stones, but no palms, no wheat.
To expand my list of minerals, I hire two Tuareg boys.

For thirty grams of couscous and a drawing lesson,
they bring me a bag of rocks. I tell them
to shield their eyes. Eager for chalcedony or agate,
I raise my hammer, then shatter the feldspar.

Pied Crow

○ 1911 ○
Tamanrasset, Hoggar, Algeria

At dawn, before my clock
calls me to toil, pied crow arrives,
jitters the thatch, pecks my roof-beam,
wakes me from dreams of foodstuffs:
gifts of bread I cannot eat, my mouth

sewn shut, a rumble that may
or may not be potatoes galumphing
down a wooden chute. Pied crow
thrashes the reeds for an insect,
a shiny bit, an edible seed. What use?

The ground is iron that I cannot sow.
The Tuareg language evades me,
on my parched tongue becomes
pied crow's bark, not human speech.
Pied crow scritches, again stirs

the reeds, and I know all my labors
as fruitless, vanities, clutching
at the wind. Be that as it may,
I choose for my morning
fodder a mouthful of praise:

for pied crow's glossy black wings,
black head, and snowy vestments.
And for the clock's hammer
(striking its tiny wire coil)
like the chambered heart

that drums beneath my breastbone.
And the goodness of this hand
rubbing my weary neck. All things
made for our use, our conversion,
our wonderment.

At the Hermitage with John of the Cross

○ 1 9 1 1 ○

Mount Asekrem, Hoggar, Algeria

I try to finish the Tuareg dictionary with Ba Hamou,
my bossy helper. Remembering that John of the Cross
fled to a plateau like this comforts me, but only a little.
The Lord, after all, sought John in that high hidden place

riddled with caves; the Lord slipped into John's cave,
and gave him kisses, pomegranate wine, the longings
of his soul. God comes to me, if at all,
not in a lover's guise, but in the unwashed rags

of Ba Hamou, who broods in my hermitage, complains
because our mush-diet does not vary. The wind is moody,
and dangerous, he insists, a petty god, ready to sweep us
from the earth. When he is happy with me, Ba Hamou

agrees to wrestle meaning from unwieldy words
that slip my grasp, like angels who refuse to bless.
My dictionary rises like a loaf. Ba Hamou pinches
the skin-folds of his belly, swears that we cannot live

on words alone. God passes through my lips
and fills my cells, not as wine (I took the last drip
in Mass last week), but as words for *crust*. And *sore gums*.
And *dried shreds of goat-meat* that I gnaw from the bone.

Sand Mites and Olive Pits

Tamanrasset, Hoggar, Algeria

*Charles devised "a rosary of love" that could be recited
by Muslims and Christians alike.*

After the Tuareg pray the rosary
that I made from olive pits,
the drought ends, rains come,
and our brittle sheaves of millet sing,
burst into leaf, a great green rejoicing
that the aphids turn to stubble and lace.
I believe there must be some holy work

for aphids to do. Even the sand mites,
I find, are glad to nibble clean
the olive pits that I bury in the sand.
After ten days, I dig up the pits,
wash them, dry them in the shade.
I wait ten more days, then I pierce
the pits with needle and string.

Stations of the Cross in Pencil and Ink

∘ 1913 ∘
Tamanrasset, Hoggar, Algeria

I say to the side of the packing crate,
"Since my colors are gone, let there be no light,
let me draw on you a dark scene. With lead,
desert ink, and a charred stick, let me create
a starless sky and gnarled trees."

And I draw: *two friends, crows, the black hour*
of night, crack of moon like an eye swollen shut,
One friend sits on the other's shoulders,
solves the cipher of the knots, then pries,
jiggles, loosens the spikes. They free Christ's
cool and abraded body, lower it onto a linen mat.

I crave what I do not have: crayons, paints,
the burgundy of a beet, the emerald of kale.

↢

And I draw on another crate:
before sunrise, women bring spices—
oil, cassia, and sweet flag, aloe and myrrh—
to perfume His decaying flesh.

Three gray women, one pencil stub.
Numb man under a washed-out sky,
I can hold or be held only if
the other hands are made of air.

Invitation

Tamanrasset, Hoggar, Algeria

Dear Br. Sébastien,

If you know a monk who may wish to join me, tell him this:

I have been alone for ten years. Infrequently, I long for a companion, the clasp of a hand, the cadences of my mother tongue.

I work with my clumsy hands, donkey legs, and crooked back. I serve as druggist for Tuareg and Haratin; porter, hosteller, and confessor for strangers. I eat like the people of Tamanrasset—barley and dates, berries, goat's milk, an occasional tomato.

I survive winds that howl, scour, sometimes freeze; sun that withers, burns, and blinds. Unceasing drought, cracks gaping in the ground like the mouths of the dead. Then the week of rain that pounds, batters, soaks, saturates, washes the earth away.

If you know some curious monk, hearty, resilient, please share with him this letter.

Stronghold

Tamanrasset, Hoggar, Algeria

Mon Père, I am ready for all, I accept all,
and this too, if I must: Jean helps me serve
Mass to myself, but he refuses to partake.
And those far light-pricks, red stars that flare,

falter, flare again: campfires of the Senussi,
rebels breaching the Hoggar's edge.
To save the Tuareg, I draft and raise
a stronghold of sheet iron and bricks—

walls pride-tall and vainglory-thick,
bullets and carbines, moat and bridge,
chapel, water-well, manuscript room.
I abandon myself to You without measure,

with infinite trust I climb the parapet, look
across the dry riverbed. I watch Dassine,
Lalla, other Tuareg women who pack fast,
flee to the mountains with children

and elders. There, they will tie their goats
to the myrtles, bed down in caves.
Foolish, they call my fortress. *A trap.*
Day-shadows spill in like clouds of ink.

I don't know when to say the hours.
Whatever You make of me, I thank You;
I thank You for these high, muddy walls,
though they cut off visitors, block the sun,

confuse the passing of time. My eyes fall
to these crabbed hands, shift to the altar,
sink again. The moon, a pale fish, chokes
on the swill at the bottom of the well.

Cricket Song

○ 1916 ○
Tamanrasset, Hoggar, Algeria

My head clangs, my skin congeals
when I imagine your final terrain:
the moldering gloom of the cave,

giant stone corking the mouth
to seal your body in—you bid me
to imitate you, even in this?

Until you rise, Love, I am useless.
Stretching in a long rectangle
of wall-shade, I pretend my hand

crumbles dank sepulchral dirt.
Listen. In the corner, one cricket
abides. Soft-shelled, tooth-white,

he chirrs his dwarfed wings,
ragged song his answer
to the absence of light.

Someone Knocks

and I fling open my door
        it isn't the man who brings my mail
but men with guns   my neighbors   Haratin
and Tuareg   joined in a *fellagha rezzou*
they wrench and tie my arms   slam me against
the wall ransack my little fort   unbind
      and fling
           my Tuareg dictionary
             my sheaves of Tuareg poetry
drag Jean from supper and his wife
               tie him beside me
tear the cross   the heart   from my robe
my chest is puny   white as glue
     my ribs like my mother's fan
my spirit an egret   my belly a roost
I feel   the breath and the burn
as my lips form   the word I choose
        and my pages scatter in the wind

A Short Sketch of
Charles de Foucauld's Life

Charles de Foucauld is remembered today as a desert hermit and missionary, and as author of "The Prayer of Abandonment," a petition of radical faith and surrender. Born in Strasbourg, France, in 1858 and raised by a wealthy Catholic family, Charles went through a season of faithlessness and hedonism as a young adult. He reconverted to Catholicism at twenty-eight and became a monk in the Order of the Cistercians of the Strict Observance. At forty-three, he was ordained as a "free priest" and permitted to establish himself in the Sahara; he hoped that "a few poor monks" would join him and that they would evangelize by "sharing down to our last mouthful of bread with every pauper, every stranger, every guest, and receiving every human being as if he were a beloved brother."

All his life, Charles tried to find an identity that would balance his zeal, curiosity, faith, and compassion. He became an artist, geographer, abolitionist, linguist, folklorist, fort-builder, and finally a martyr. His incessant search for a vocation took him to Algeria as a cavalry officer in his early twenties; to Morocco as a clandestine explorer posing as a Jewish rabbi; to monasteries in France and then Syria; to the Holy Land, where he worked as a gardener for a convent of Poor Clares; and at last, back to Algeria. Here, he settled in Béni Abbès, a thriving oasis town not far from the Moroccan border. He opened his home to "all comers" and called it "a *zaouïa* [fraternity] of prayer and hospitality"; he wrote, "I want to accustom all the inhabitants, be they Christians, Muslims, Jews or nonbelievers, to see me as their brother, a universal brother." Later, Charles moved south and lived in the Hoggar, a mountainous region in the central Sahara whose Tuareg inhabitants seemed warlike, dangerous, poor, and marginalized. As an expression of humility and solidarity, he wore a *gandoura* like the Tuareg, ate barley and dates like the Tuareg, and studied their language. Over time, he collected Tuareg proverbs and poems, translated the Gospels, and devised a "rosary of love" for both Muslim Tuaregs and Christians to pray. On December 1, 1916, he was assassinated by rebels during the Senussi revolt, and was beatified by Pope Benedict XVI on November 13, 2005. He is remembered as a martyr for his faith.

Although Charles failed to make converts or establish a monastery in his lifetime, his rule of silence, contemplative prayer, and selfless compassion inspired the founding of the Little Brothers and the Little Sisters of Jesus. As Thomas Merton observes, "his formula for the 'contemplative' life seems simply to have been to go off into the desert and become, for all practical purposes, a Tuareg." Devoting himself to self-denial, adoration, silence, and charity, Charles claimed the nomadic Tuareg as his brothers, the desert as his earthly home.

Chronology

1 8 5 8 Charles de Foucauld is born in Strasbourg, France.

1 8 6 4 After the death of his parents, Edouard and Elisabeth, Charles and his sister live with his maternal grandfather, Colonel Charles de Morlet.

1 8 7 4 Charles attends Jesuit and military schools in Paris and Guer, drifts from his childhood faith, and gains a reputation for gluttony, drunkenness, and seducing women.

1 8 8 0 While serving as a cavalry officer in Algeria, Charles comes to love North Africa.

1 8 8 3 Disguised as a Jewish rabbi, Charles explores Morocco; he crosses the Rif and Atlas Mountains, reaching the Sous Valley. Stirred by the faith of Moroccan Muslims who live "always in the presence of God," Charles begins to ponder "something greater and more real than the pleasures of this world."

1 8 8 5 Charles returns to Paris, writes *Reconnaissance au Maroc*, and receives a gold medal from the French Geographical Society. His wealth and achievements do not satisfy him. He prays, "My God, if you exist, make your existence known to me."

1 8 8 6 Upon receiving communion from Father Henri Huvelin in the Saint-Augustin Church, Charles reconverts to Catholicism.

1 8 9 0 Charles joins Our Lady of the Snows, a Cistercian-Trappist monastery in France; at his request, he receives a transfer to a more austere monastery in Syria.

1 8 9 7   Charles relocates to Nazareth in the Holy Land, where he lives
          as the gardener of a Poor Clares convent. The mother superior
          encourages him to become a priest and to consider founding a
          monastic community.

1 9 0 1   After studying for the priesthood at Our Lady of the Snows and
          receiving ordination in Viviers, Charles settles in Béni Abbès,
          an oasis and garrison town in the northern Sahara Desert.

1 9 0 5   Charles moves south to the Hoggar to work as a missionary and
          translator among the Tuareg and the Haratin.

1 9 0 7   During a season of famine and drought, Charles and his
          neighbors share with each other their diminishing stores
          of food.

1 9 1 0   Charles builds a hermitage on Mount Assekreme and works on
          the Tuareg dictionary there.

1 9 1 5   Charles pays several Haratin workers to build a fort for the
          protection of the local community.

1 9 1 6   Charles is murdered by Tuareg and Haratin raiders during the
          Senussi uprising.

Acknowledgments

Assisi	Village Martyr
Blackbird	My Father as Weather Formation, My Mother as Harp Seal, as Sacristan
Cheat River Review	The Skin of a Viper's Jaw Transfigured
The Christian Century	Cricket Song
Christianity and Literature	King of Hush, Sparrow Lament
Cimarron Review	Obedientiary
The Freeman	We Hide Our Faces from the Wind
Grey Sparrow	The Hamidian Massacres
The Hollins Critic	Gourd Seeds
Hotel Amerika	Automaton with Flute
Image	Liturgy of the Hours
LETTERS	Brother Almost, Stronghold
The Literary Bohemian	Teresa of Avila Compares the Soul to a Palm Cabbage, Invitation
Nimrod	Oasis Prayers, Words for Flesh
Paper Nautilus	Red Coals
Pebble Lake Review	Summer in Giverny
Pilgrimage	For Three Hundred Francs, Body as Pomegranate Tree, Skin Tent
qarrtsiluni	Seed Speck, Tuber Eye
Redivider	Flight Lines
Rhino	Memento
Seminary Ridge Review	Changeling
Saint Katherine Review	Gold Eater, The Pangs of Wanting, Stations of the Cross in Pen and Ink
Salamander	Christmas at the Frigate (i)
Sou'wester	Desert Bath at Sunset
Spiritus	Blue Aster, Consider the Ant, Pied Crow
Thrush	At the Ruins of Pilate's Palace
Tiferet	The Children's Book of the Nativity
Tiger's Eye	Meditation on the Hands of an Ex-Slave
The Wayfarer	Cavalry Scene, The Rope Maker, At the Hermitage with John of the Cross
White Whale Review	The House of Bones, To Map the Land of God, Confessions of an Illuminator, Dust and Oil
Windhover	Sand Mites and Olive Pits, Hornet Swarm as the Sins of Mankind

About Paraclete Press

WHO WE ARE

Paraclete Press is a publisher of books, recordings, and DVDs on Christian spirituality. Our publishing represents a full expression of Christian belief and practice—from Catholic to Evangelical, from Protestant to Orthodox.

We are the publishing arm of the Community of Jesus, an ecumenical monastic community in the Benedictine tradition. As such, we are uniquely positioned in the marketplace without connection to a large corporation and with informal relationships to many branches and denominations of faith.

WHAT WE ARE DOING

Paraclete Press Books

Paraclete publishes books that show the richness and depth of what it means to be Christian. Although Benedictine spirituality is at the heart of all that we do, we publish books that reflect the Christian experience across many cultures, time periods, and houses of worship. We publish books that nourish the vibrant life of the church and its people.

We have several different series, including the best-selling Paraclete Essentials and Paraclete Giants series of classic texts in contemporary English; Voices from the Monastery—men and women monastics writing about living a spiritual life today; award-winning poetry; best-selling gift books for children on the occasions of baptism and first communion; and the Active Prayer Series that brings creativity and liveliness to any life of prayer.

Mount Tabor Books

Paraclete's newest series, Mount Tabor Books, focuses on liturgical worship, art and art history, ecumenism, and the first millennium church, and was created in conjunction with the Mount Tabor Ecumenical Centre for Art and Spirituality in Barga, Italy.

Paraclete Recordings

From Gregorian chant to contemporary American choral works, our recordings celebrate the best of sacred choral music composed through the centuries that create a space for heaven and earth to intersect. Paraclete Recordings is the record label representing the internationally acclaimed choir Gloriæ Dei Cantores, praised for their "rapt and fathomless spiritual intensity" by *American Record Guide*; the Gloriæ Dei Cantores Schola, specializing in the study and performance of Gregorian chant; and the other instrumental artists of the Gloriæ Dei Artes Foundation.

Paraclete Press is also privileged to be the exclusive North American distributor of the recordings of the Monastic Choir of St. Peter's Abbey in Solesmes, France, long considered to be a leading authority on Gregorian chant.

Paraclete Video

Our DVDs offer spiritual help, healing, and biblical guidance for a broad range of life issues including grief and loss, marriage, forgiveness, facing death, bullying, addictions, Alzheimer's, and spiritual formation.

99 Psalms

○   S A I D   ○

Translated by Mark S. Burrows

ISBN: 978-1-61261-294-2, $17.99, Paperback

These are poems of praise and lament, of questioning and wondering. In the tradition of the Hebrew psalmist, they find their voice in exile, in this case one that is both existential and geographical.

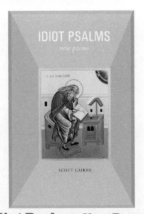

Idiot Psalms: New Poems

○   S C O T T   C A I R N S   ○

ISBN: 978-1-61261-515-8, $17.00, Paperback

A new collection from one of our favorite poets. Fourteen "Idiot Psalms," surrounded by dozens of other poems, make this his most challenging collection yet.

Eyes Have I That See

○ JOHN JULIAN ○

ISBN: 978-1-61261-640-7, $18.00, Paperback

From rough folk-verse to high-flown poesy, from a nine-line rhyme to a six-hundred-line epic, both the style and genre of the poetry in this volume cover a broad range of poetic possibility. This is the first volume of John Julian's poetry ever published, revealing an important new American poetic voice.

Available from most booksellers or through Paraclete Press: www.paracletepress.com | 1-800-451-5006
Try your local bookstore first.